JESUS THESIS AND OTHER CRITICAL FABULATIONS

JESUS THESIS
AND OTHER CRITICAL FABULATIONS

POEMS BY

KOPANO MAROGA

UHLANGA

2020

First published in Durban, South Africa by uHlanga in 2020
UHLANGAPRESS.CO.ZA

Distributed outside southern Africa by the African Books Collective
AFRICANBOOKSCOLLECTIVE.COM

ISBN: 978-1-990968-65-5

Edited by Nick Mulgrew
Cover images by Elijah Ndoumbé (ELIJAHNDOUMBE.COM)
Cover design and typesetting by Nick Mulgrew
Collages by Kopano Maroga
Proofread by Jennifer Jacobs and Karina Szczurek

The body text of this book is set in Garamond Premier Pro 11PT on 15PT

NOTES & ACKNOWLEDGEMENTS

I want to start by thanking my family, both biological and found, for shoring me up in so many different ways through the currents of my life and also this book: my mother Nomvuselelo Pemba, my father Jacob Maroga, and my siblings, Sello and Reatliwe. Special thanks go to my dear friends and lovers who have held this book with me in one way or another: Mlondiwethu Dubazane, Nomi Blum, Cullan Maclear, Mmakhotso Lamola, Jan Wallyn, Luvuyo Equiano Nyawose, Maneo Mohale, Dani Kyengo O'Neill, Lindiwe Mngxitama, Nonhle Skosana, Jesse Navarre Vos, Ugo Woatzi, Brooklyn Dahmer, and Elijah Ndoumbé. This would never have been possible without all of you.

I want to send a huge thank you to Nick Mulgrew at uHlanga for believing in these poems, for your attentive and questioning eye in the editing process and for following me through this journey with curiosity and a cultivating hand. Your contribution to what this book has become is immeasurable.

The images in this book were made in collaboration with the following photographers: Elijah Ndoumbé on the front and back cover, the author's portrait, and page 74; Jesse Navarre Vos on pages 12, 26, 31, 42, and 62–63; Ugo Woatzi on page 67; and Brooklyn Dahmer on page 89. The warmest of thanks to you all for birthing this project with me in so many different iterations.

"ode to brandon cody ending in a rainstorm of flowers" and "nectar" were first published in a special edition publication for Bâtard festival in Brussels, Belgium, and later in the inaugural edition of *Kabaka* magazine, founded by Chibuihe Achimba and Romeo Oriogun in late 2018. "jesus thesis" would also form part of the first edition of *Kabaka* – thanks go to Pieter Odendaal for editing the works with such care. "at swim, two boys" first appeared in volume 11 of *20:35 Africa: An Anthology of Contemporary Poetry,* with thanks to guest editors, Yasmin Belkhyr and Kayo Chingonyi, and their team.

This body of work comes out of my Master of Arts in Interdisciplinary Studies in Public Spheres and Performance Studies at the University of Cape Town. Huge thanks are extended to the Institute for Creative Arts, with whom I was an MA fellow, and the Centre for Theatre, Dance and Performance Studies through which I obtained my qualification and to the Andrew Mellon Foundation who funded my studies. A very special thanks to my supervisors Jay Pather and Mbongeni Mtshali, for your guidance, mentorship and provocation through this process. I am so appreciative of you both, through shade and through scholarship!

Thank you, God, for making me a seed and planting me in such rich soil.

– K.M.

CONTENTS

"If God is omnipotent and omnipresent then everything is a prayer."

– JULIE NXADI

for judas

MAN OF SORROWS,
A TENDER SHOOT

Though much is known about the early childhood of Jesus of Nazareth and his ministry from his late twenties, there are no historical documents that help us divine with certainty just where and what our dear Lord and Saviour was up to between the ages of twelve and twenty-nine: *The Lost Years of Jesus*.

Some scholars posit that it was most probable that he was apprenticing with his father, Joseph, as a carpenter. In the late medieval period there appeared Arthurian legends that the young Jesus had been in Britain. In the 19th and 20th centuries, theories began to emerge that Jesus had visited Kashmir instead, or had studied with the Essenes in the Judea desert.

And, yet, there exists another theory for how Jesus spent those years...

jesus was a faggot
jesus liked it rough
jesus was a masochist
jesus liked whips and chains
(sometimes nails)
jesus had a safe word
no one remembers it
no one dares try

jesus was femme
jesus had wrists so limp
they had to nail them straight
send him to conversion therapy
jesus didn't make it
jesus' mother wept
jesus' mother wept
jesus' mother wept

jesus was a drag queen
jesus served face
for   the   gods
jesus had a drag name
jesus had many drag names:
jehovah gyrate
jehovah nississy
jehovah shame-lom

prince of penises
prince in pieces

jesus was a power bottom
jesus had daddy issues
jesus was a dzaddy
jesus was an otter
jesus was a cum slut
a holy ghost covered in semen
jesus let so many men inside of him
he became an ocean

his lovers
fishers of men

jesus didn't know how to make boundaries
jesus practiced ethical polyamory
he gave until there was nothing left of him
and on the day he disappeared
his body became a tomb
and jesus wept
god, jesus wept

————————
jesus thesis

I.
have you heard the one
about the boi who cried wolf?
their tears laid into their flesh
until there was nothing left but bone

      what they will not tell you about grief
      is that it hunts in packs
      hunts to kill!
      stalks its prey with carnivorous intent

II.
once upon a once, all their sadness would collect
in their back: a nest of glass encasing a spine
such a body can be many things
every piece in an armoire of fine china

III.

in the world that is not this one
all the crushed glass in their back
transmutes into crystalline feathers. they are
sainted: the winged patron of grieving wolves

    a howl to the moon
    a clarion call for every ghost left haunted
        back into your graves!
    even the dead need rest

    in the world that is not this one
    we will stalk the plains of our suffering and
    call every sadness by its name
    make a meal in this tundra

    we will eat until we are full
    and weep until we are drowned

          wings

holy holy holy bottle
holy blackout
holy four hours of sleep
holy headache
holy light of day
holy hangover
holy pill after pill after pill after
holy unravelling
holy drunk before midday
holy ghost
holy take me to the place where judas kissed jesus
holy i want to remember what he tasted like
holy turn my water into wine
holy paint my face with your holy seed
holy keep me on my knees
holy fuck me sanctified
holy fuck me happy
holy fuck me normal
holy help me make it through another day

amen
again
again, amen

morning eucharist

glory to the meek
glory to the body trodden underfoot
glory to the soft light of mourning
beckoning us ever heavenward

glory to the silence and the outrage
the quiet violence that dare not speak its name
but speaks ours in our darkest hour
and says our time is spent

       oh! but the sleeplessness!
       the heartache!
       generations of it pooling at our feet!
       a Red Sea with no parting!

             they don't know
          when you shoot a black body
           you shoot an invocation
           //hands up don't shoot//
           a nexus of clapping hands
           //hands up don't shoot//
            a conjuring of spirits
           //hands up don't shoot//
             a wellspring
           //hands up don't shoot//
      that the blood that spills is holy water
           //hands up don't shoot//   ↘

they don't know of the joy and the bellyache and the burial grounds
and the ring-shout and the waking fear and the restless bones and the
withering spines and the ancestors and the sacrifice and the give and
the gift and the grief that has no name but will swallow yours whole

they don't know the price of the ticket and yet they still want to ride

my mother has a voice
my father has a face
when i was born they named me unity so that they will never be apart
and i can know that should all else fail i have earned my namesake

the work:
to love unconditionally
to love unendingly
i only have love so i give it unsparingly

until my chest is empty and i am collapsing into my self in parts
then the god of small things takes me and breaks me
and there is more love to give
glory to the miracle of love that is unceasing

to know that the cup runs over
and when it is emptied will be filled again
glory to the miracle of two hands
one for receiving and one for letting go

glory to the humility that meekness brings
glory to the knees that cannot straighten
there is a seat for you at the table of the undying
and when they come for you

let them know that you have known good love and
have loved well and therefore have nothing to fear
let them know how your voice was a piercing
cry all through the black night of your existence

that the tears fell even when unbeckoned
that you unzipped your sternum and made
of yourself a safe haven and would not let
any frail thing be turned away

let them know that you were broken bread and spilt wine
      holy! holy! holy!
thrice blessed and thrice favoured
let them know that where they bury you there will grow seeds

<hr>

griefsong

if i don't ask, you
need not tell.
      i thought i could
      get away with this.

if you close your eyes at the precise
moment of a car crash would
everybody make it out alive?
      i thought i could get away with this.

memory is the closest thing we
have to viable human cryonics.
we, who should be
halfway to colonising Mars by now.

we, who were promised flying
cars and now can barely wake
up in the mornings enough to wade
through what it is we have done here.

if i closed my eyes at the time
everything was said and done,
maybe there would be less
pills on my kitchen counter. less pages

spilling over with why
why why why

i promise,
there is a world in which we
did not unseam each other.

i promise,
there is a world in which we
were only good to one another.

i promise,
there is a world in which i
sleep through the night and
you never left and
i never yelled and
nothing broke and
there is no scar tissue and
we are not still mending

i promise,
but it is not this one

---

don't ask

this is how it happens:
a disappearance
a sock in the laundry
a sternum that leaks

the dam wall breaks
and we never swim again
never dare to dip our toes into
the infinite possibility of drowning

every body of water is a burial
who would know sustenance if not for scarcity?
who would know presence
without his shadow absence?

i'm trying to say something profound here about loss
but if you know the thing you know the thing
and you know:

>> *you're gonna carry that weight!*

from Calvary to Galilee

---

in the desert you cannot cry

sometimes i am so lonely
even my chest bone
echoes
the problem being that
       wherever i go
this haunted body
goes with

epithet

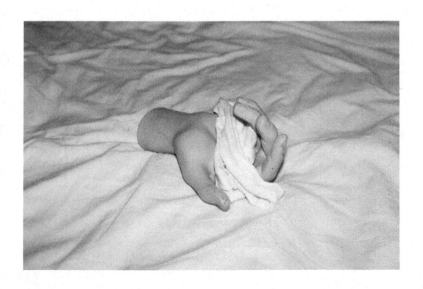

i cannot count love without loss
live without death
tip without a calculator
some things just go together

loud as sunlight through the curtains
on all the mornings that saw me
weeping the night through
some things just go together

my hand in between my own fingers now
reaching for the phantom flat of your back
or the spectral curl of your hair
against my forehead

that you made a mountain
how you took my sternum for a cliff face
your forearms so good for climbing
for slicing oranges into morbid grins

the hemispheres of my brain humming something like apocalypse
learning to breathe with my mouth closed
calling the drowning body Atlantis
and all the ones before us queens and kings

there is no need to grieve the undying
there is no where to bury that which lives on
call it intergenerational trauma
or the faint cry of a people not yet done living

sodom and gomorrah

and so it was winter
so i was starving
so every mouthful
was a   rationed miracle
every raindrop a flood

so it was take anything
    at arm's reach   and pull
so it was cut down the trees
build the boat
take the animals   two by two

when you live like this
you can survive on the absence
of your own longing
    i would count the hours
the nights

the shadows
how much more hunger
there was of me than me
        an echo with no sound
i named my hands after something biblical

and everything they touched: ash
everywhere my feet lay: salt
everything dredged up from the sea bed:
                    lost, lost, lost

---

lot's wife and the name we forgot

gorge (*noun*):
      a full empty, a sharp open
      gorge (*verb*):
      to fill, to fall, to flail,
      to break with full filling

i can't write like i used to
not with everything lying under
this sheet of alcoholic hum
nothing vibrating but everything
      hum, hum, hum
like the refrigerator in the night
or the washing machine spilling
over its own load

sorry liver
sorry kidney
sorry ascending and descending colon
sorry thrice holy body:
thrice forgotten
thrice milk spilt
thrice split lip
thrice opening and opening and opening   ↙

i've always loved the word gorge
the shape your mouth has
to make to say it
the emptiness it leaves in its wake
as though making space for itself
to fill itself with its own absence
the idea of something so filled with
nothing it warranted a word

    a disappearance so complete
    it took on materiality

————————————————

and it shall be opened unto you

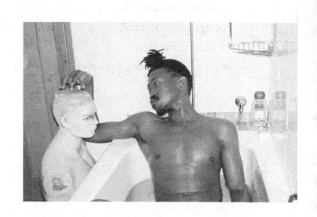

1. (EGG)
take your trauma / your trauma takes you
what are you left with
the age old question
of what came first
you or your trauma / your trauma or you

II. (STAIRWAY)
i think i'll need a skylight
a pair of scissors and some
willing flesh
a boy with
too-big hands
something dark
behind his
irises

i think i'll get down on
my knees again and
find that old tongue rattling
back to life under my
soft palate
rustling like hymnal pages as they
hummingbird in church

i think i'll tell god about
the hard season
how i went scratching through the
topography of my body
like some crazed archaeologist
looking for ruins
for something that this world had long forgotten ↘

III.

look dad, i'm a monument!
it's true
animate testament to colonial contact
a vector without pause
look, i'll prove it
pry open my jaw and dare tell me you
don't see all these glimmering
white teeth
shining brighter than the
queen's kitchen set

and you know she knows a thing or two
about polishing stolen silver
until all it can do is shine
until all she can do is scream
       mine!
and god be damned if i am
not a quick learner
god be damned if i
didn't see what it would mean
for me to survive my life

and live anyway
god be damned!

_____

(don't you know) even uncle tom gets the blues

i have so many secrets:
a collection for each
season. when spring comes
around i turn sour in my

own sweet. a mess of
sweat and spit and *please,*
please, please! summer is for
hunger. i eat until i throw up,

lick the floor clean until
the leaves start turning amber
and i can lie still under
blankets of bloody handprints.

in winter i dream of the
shadows becoming so long
i can cross them into the
underworld. i count my

blessings and chalk up another
death. it's oh so quiet, i can
ask the questions that i don't
dare to ask under the sun's light:

1.   how do i *feel* after this?
2.   how do i crawl back into the
      cave of my body and 3.   light a
      fire for the heat and not the burn?   ↘

to say it plainly, i *am*
bursting with my own
want! reeking! wanting a
dick inside of me for

a hunger with no axis!
　　　　a mouth by any other name
　　　　would be just as sweet. a mouth
　　　　by any other name would be just... sweet

there's a less complicated way
to say this. i think it starts with
fuck and ends with *me*. i want you
to end in me. horizon to sun

set. dusk to dawn. seed to
harvest. if we pull the grain from
the ground at just the right time, if the
grain can be ground into meal, meal

into flour. we might have enough
bread to see us through this interminable
famine. there might be something
like life after love. an unconsecrated

sacrament. so, yes: holy spirit, mother
mary, soft god(dess) of the erection,
warrior of the wet tongue, apostle of
gaping assholes, i am asking for

it. on my knees; tongue
outstretched. i am begging to be
fed on bread and bread
                    alone

_____

                    touch hungry & leaking

some things don't change
i still drink wine straight from the bottle
just like B_____ taught me
said,

>   *this is how the brazilians do it*

a habit borrowed from his south american lover
and,
now,
a secret i'd meant to keep for myself

>   no matter

the best secrets are the ones you can't keep
and besides
how else would i know how much time has passed
if i couldn't mark it with another alcoholic stumble
down memory lane

>   *i wish i could be more creative with my grief*
but the best secrets
are the ones you can't keep
so let this be something of an ad hoc
eucharist: the body broken for you

my body broken for you
again and again and again and
damn it
i can still feel your hair
underneath my fingertips

maybe this time

> *yes*
i have wrist bones made
of glass
> *no*
nothing, and yet everything,
has broken
> *maybe*
tomorrow is a place where we can
store the splintered pieces
> *might*
be time to start counting
the window panes again

> *an exit*
>> also a way to find
>> another welcome
> *home*
>> nowhere closer than
>>> it was before
> *i*
>> don't believe in
>>> the future
> *but*
>> i give it everything i
>>> can carry

> *in these*

>>>> my two hands made
>>>> for shaking

———————

temperance

i was made a punchline
before i could become
a person, and, though a
victim, i have also
been a perpetrator

disgraced and
dethroned, i
wear a crown
with many thorns

jesus wept

ROSE OF SHARON,
FLOWER OF THE FIELD

Let me tell you of that which I have lost so I might
sew an ever unfurling sea of sunflowers
from these pits of Hades
I, the Morning Star
I, the Queen of Heaven
Sister to Ereshkigal
I, Maris Stella
I, lover of Ares
Wife of Joseph
Mother of Hermaphroditus
Born of the severed genitals of Uranus, Father Sky
I, the many-faced spectre of love
Second planet from the sun
Call me by name
Kgoshigadi ya Legodimo. Mma wa Modimo
That which was smothered to death in the
ivory chamber of my mouth at birth
And rises stillborn at every utterance
of my mother's tongue
I who have descended to the underworld
Stripped and struck dead
My body hung from a hook
my disgrace for all and sundry to behold
My shame a spectacle

I, Ishtar
I, Inanna
I, Afroditi
I, Isis
I, Venus
I, Ọsun
I, Mariá
I, _____
I, _____
I, _____

my mother used to grow roses!

above our heads. in the
old garden where i think she
was happiest, or, as close
as she could get and

my mother used to grow roses!

tall and brambled and wild and
peeking over the neighbour's wall and
honey-humming and
full to bursting and

my mother used to grow roses!

and her fingers for thorns and
her throat for a stem and
my throat choked quiet and
the beatings! the beatings! the beatings!

my mother used to grow roses!

and my father's hand slicing
through my brother's face like
frosted birthday cake through
smiling children's lips and

my mother used to grow roses!

and sometimes i would scream
when she would hit me: thunder and rain
without a cloud in sight. but as i got older
i found a place to store them for winter and

my mother used to grow roses!

and my body: all static. my body: all
rumbling sky. my body: a placeholder, a
metaphor, a phantasma of a grief not of my
own making but threatening to unmake me and

my mother used to grow roses!

tall and brambled and ████ and
████████████████████████ and
████████████ and
████████████ and

they don't seem to grow at all anymore

in my mother's garden

no

not *gay* as in happy but
queer as in chronic depression
avoidant attachment
social anxiety
fear of the sidewalk
fear of the shadow men
of the shadows of men
of my shadow who has a man's hunger
of my own hands with their ceaseless longing

my *gay* is the quiet unflowering
of my sex
is the smell of fresh lube and
ruptured condom wrappers
left under beds, under fingers, in the palm of your hand
as i press my tongue into it

my *gay* is the way i bend at the waist
but don't break
until you let me
until you open me up like a crack of teeth
straight through a jawbreaker
straight to the sweet and the stick
and i say several silent prayers that
your unwrapped cock
will not make me a cliché
will not prove my mother right about us
and how we always meet our ends
too sick and too soon

no

not tonight
tonight i am all fear and eyes wide
tonight you are daddy and i am the boi with
my ass up on your sofa
falling to pieces
falling into and onto your thickness
until we are both drowned men

flower boy fuck me gently

can you peel the petals from my eyes
it would take nothing less than this

follow the contour of my stem and
bite into anything that would

give you sustenance enough to
survive the dry lands

do you understand
i am blooming only for you

i am blooming only for you
do you understand

the pollen is just a ruse
unpetal me soft as a rosebud

reveal what lies thereunder and
say it's everything you've been praying for

do you understand
it can be soft and sudden

bud to bloom

maybe through the granary of young love
maybe there where everything was a first blossoming

i remember J_____ and
his soft brown eyes and
the laugh that lay like
a pearl in his clam-tight mouth
his big boyhands
his arms so good for
holding and
folding into
i remember a
heavenly and heady hemorrhaging

i remember a boy speaking my name and
turning me to leaves in autumn
windstruck and branchless
then there were the nights L___ would
curve himself to fit the length of my spine
as if to say,
i would like to hold the memory of
your body so close that your absence will
be just another form of presence
and that night with my arms making
concentric circles on M_____'s back
his spine long enough to
climb a stairway to heaven   ↘

i tell myself memory is like this
a good place to visit but
not to stay

wanderlust

i knelt at every altar
prayed to any god who would listen
idolatrous in my ravings
i called death by all her names
i was ravenous and reeking of something
spoilt and sinister
sleep wouldn't answer
but when it came left me hollow
my innards clutching that other shore
carved out i beseeched the ground
to swallow me and let me lay
like a dormant bulb
gluttonous with my un-blossoming
full to bursting with untapped nectar

beka ilitye

the blossom knows not the violence
it has done unto the bud
this is what it means to bloom
to rupture that which you were
before your
                b l o o m i n g
    in the summer
                the evenings are heavy set
                        with the cries of the cicada
a funeral dirge
thick with pollen

---

someone i love asked me for the definition of humidity
and all i got was this unshakeable grief

the first time i came
i think i must have been seven
envisioning someone
with pamela anderson's body
but no face
hands like hummingbirds
overflowing nectar
a torrential springtime

this was before sex
this was before shame
before a life of watching myself
perform myself
for an audience of hands
flesh hard
flesh desperate
flesh trying to fuck itself into oblivion

the memory of that
impossible springtime
brings more grief
than there are graves to bury it

————

nectar

Brandon:
   paragon of pleasure
      palimpsest of youth's eternal flower
         polemic portent of vociferous longing

there are few things more quintessentially
growing-up-gay-on-tumblr than the image of
gay porn star Brandon Cody on his knees,
eyes heavenward, getting a facial from Marshall:

     a eucharist for one

this, our unholy iconography
this, our baby Jesus and Madonna
him, on his knees in worship
his eyes aglow as the cum rains
manna-like from Marshall's cock
     the lord be with you

     ...and also with you

Brandon: moniker of gay disciplehood
Brandon: brown-haired and tan-skinned
Brandon: white and unfettered by preference and positionality
Brandon: patron saint of the six-packed and green-eyed

Brandon,
when i realised i could never be you
all i wanted was to have you

Brandon,
you are there in every sexual encounter and
i want them all back

Brandon: true north
Brandon: statue of david
Brandon: creation of adam
Brandon: apocryphal adonis

i told my therapist
            i feel like my sexual flower is wilting
and
besides it harkening back to
that image of the rose wilting
underneath the glass in *Beauty & the Beast*
        a pantomime of
        time and disrepair
it was accurate
with enough exposure
anything will decay
there is something in me that is wilted
there is something in me
that refuses to bloom again

Brandon,
        i want to tell you that there are few images
            more beautiful in my adolescent memory
                than you in that solitary rainstorm   ⬎

Brandon,
i cannot tell you how indescribably sad that makes me

Brandon,
there is a secret flower somewhere in this world

Brandon,
i don't know if i will ever find it

---

ode to brandon cody ending in a rainstorm of flowers

and, in full bloom we wake to find   the dawn is still singing

and my mother   calls
and she is still   weeping
whether from   joy or grief i can't
hear through   the static

the continents are   still drifting
we call it   a homecoming
when the shores   meet
and when   they rupture
we call this   a beginning

and our people are   no longer dying
but now   finally
                                        resting

we name their bones   something like forever
                                        something like almost

and we are   floating
with our bodies forever   opening towards the sky
which could be a mouth   full of our leaving

and we call this   today
which is a place to leave   anything like sorrow

it brings us great joy   and even greater pain
to know that the end is   something we can never enter
but only hurtle   towards

we call this the river
for what it means to
yet to always be

and the river is a good teacher
never go back
returning

we call this an
because somewhere there is
but was always

ending
a door that cannot be opened
ours to search for

we call this
for all that we have lost

a benediction
while we were in our searching

and like this
in an orchard of fruit

we are an unblooming
too ripe for the harvest

---

a benediction

let us begin anywhere, as we must begin somewhere

scene one
there was the night with my spine
curled in towards your stomach
less like spooning and more like
the crescent moon and its shadow

scene two
you look at me like the secret of
flowers is blooming just behind my irises
spring is always a welcome season
in a world so honey-hungry

scene three
i ran you a bath and dressed it in petals and oils
watched your nakedness protruding
i kept my eyes down
my breath quiet

scene four
the couch and the pills and the nights we couldn't sleep but were
    empty of crying
the cheese and egg sandwiches
something silently feasting on us both
neither of us knowing how to make it stop; neither of us knowing
    how to make it stop

scene five
i imprinted my lips onto yours on a balcony on Long Street
because i love you and you love me and this is what
two people in the golden room do
i can't remember the taste but i remember your eyes

scene six
you disappeared

scene seven

scene eight
the darkness will always hold us

scene nine
i still remember

marco, polo

it's true i've seen the end of days
and there were no pearly gates
but there was fire, everything we lost
piles and piles of mismatched socks

i thought adulthood would
come with more interesting problems
i'm still trying to figure out how
to get the boys on the playground to like me

still rocking myself into stasis
taste of soccer field soil
taste of blood flowing from the nose
taste of knee to the face

taste of folded limbs and
something soft being rendered silent
this is where it ends
this is where we begin

to unlock the heart is
to unravel grief
ripe and unplucked
an ever unfurling bud

can you imagine it?
the tight fist settling into a hand fit for holding
maybe the heart wants to be held
let the cycle complete

inside me: an unholy cryogenesis
the embryo of a younger me
lain to rest in the tomb of my chest
something man made myth

something god made man

---

instructions for opening the heart

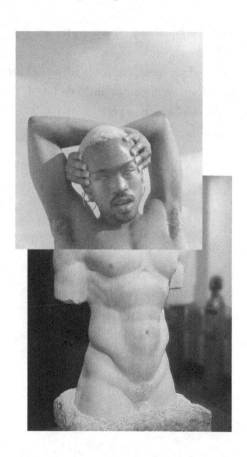

things begin to shift and increasingly
there are fewer flowers that choose to bloom
the air is not how it used to be
i don't get to touch you with my hands
i ask stranger questions:

did i leave the paints in the box or in my ribcage?
when will you remember that there are good things about me too?
was there always a wall here?
when did i get so fucking lonely?
why won't you love me like i want?

i did the equations
i did the legwork
i turned my mouth into a holding cell for silence
and now i want you to lie down beside me and love me
it doesn't have to be real
but it has to be now

I JUST WANT MY BODY BACK

slow puncture

i once fashioned a man out of nothing more
than an idea and acute desperation
loneliness is akin to godliness
and isn't that a beautiful way to deify my condition
more island than shipwreck
more blue moon than starlight

spectres

i wanted a million sunrises
i wanted a man with sunflowers for hands
i wanted an eternal horizon we could run to
hands clasped firm as the dying light clutching the mountains

and i wanted to lie with him until
we were nothing but bone
i wanted archaeologists to try and fail to divine from
the silt of the earth how a love like that could survive

i wanted to lie in the dirt for centuries
whispering pebbled fables
i wanted to feel the universe pulverise us into something quartz-like
    and glimmering
something so sinful in its sanctity they would make a secret of us

i wanted a myth more ancient than the earth itself
something post-entropy
something pre-primordial
can you imagine?

the love stories the stars are
trying to flicker to us from space
how many asteroids are trying to collide
into the parts of themselves they have lost

the genesis of the universe is
the cosmic love story never told
there is not enough dark matter to hold up
this much space

i want him back!

i sing a song for the man on the moon
hoping he remembers the tune

let love be a field of asteroids

i've mostly been focusing on
trying not to die, which, for the
most part, has been a successful
endeavour, thanks for asking.

every hour: a day, every day:
an eternity. every hour-on-the-
hour: another departure;
another impossible agony.

i stopped counting so
long ago... where would
we pick it up again?
from the first blowjob or the

last kiss? from my tongue tracing
the petals of your asshole, or
the scream in the pillow,
or the pre-cum still slick on

your kitchen floor? *remember,*
remember, that night in november?
solange crooning though your
speakers and me, drunk as ever?

i promise, i'm not holding
out just holding on until
this wave rides itself out.
call me grief surfer or

depression trawler. call me
anything other than by your
name. call me a year from now
and tell me how it was me. how

i ruined it all with my stupid
sausage fingers: all over you. call
me boundary-crossed. call me the
line as i walked over it. crossed out.

i don't want to feel this
way, i promise. i'm just
not creative enough to
make it up as i go along any

> *more! more! more!*
> *how do you like it?*
> *how do you like it?*
> *more! more! more!*

——————————

more! more! more!

IMMANUEL,
WONDERFUL IN COUNSEL

I Am (Exodus 3:14)...

Iēsūs, Yēšūă, First Begotten (Revelation 1:5), Collins Khosa (04.2020), Sibusiso Amos (29.03.2020) Desire of the Nations (Haggai 2:7), Good Shepherd (John 10:11), Uyinene Mrwetyana (29.08.2020), Immanuel (Isaiah 7:14), Marielle Franco (14.03.2018), Lamb of God (John 1:29), Gift of God (2 Corinthians 9:15), Mawda Shawri (17.05.2018), Man of Sorrows (Isaiah 53:3), Sandra Bland (13.07.2015), Morning Star (Revelation 22:16), Sikhosiphi Bazooka Rhadebe (22.03.2016), Light of the World (John 8:12; John 9:5), Petrus Miggels (27.03.2020), Nare Mphela (05.01.2020), Only Begotten Son (John 1:18), George Floyd (25.05.2020), Rose of Sharon (Song of Songs 2:1), Horn of Salvation (Luke 1:69), Adil (10.04.2020), Lorena Xtravaganza (05.12.2012),

Foundation (Isaiah 28:16), Resurrection (John 11:25), Mgcineni Noki (16.08.2012), Sacrifice (Ephesians 5:2), Saviour (2 Samuel 22:47; Luke 1:47); Jehovah-jireh: My Provider; Jehovah-nissi: Lord you reign in victory; Jehovah-shalom: My prince of peace.
My prince in pieces.

I.

where do we begin
where do we begin

i end where my gender begins:
in 1652 / with a boat
with many boats / with many many ghosts
we begin where...

where
where

in the languages of my mother's and
father's tongues there is no pronoun for
he or she / only: you / only: them / only: me

where do we begin
where do we begin

in the language of my mother's and
father's tongues we call people by their names
we do not call people by the secret flower we imagine
may or may not be blooming between their thighs

where do we begin
where do we begin

↘

in the land of my mother's and
father's tongues we have the
fourth highest rate of
femicide in the world

    where do we begin
    where do we begin

in the country of my mother's
and father's tongues we have lost
so much and there is no
one to count the bodies

    where do we begin
    where do we begin

in the country of my mother's
and father's tongues there is a
burning roof and no one to
sing the smoke to sleep

    where do we begin
    where do we begin

II.

in the new world my tongue is pink and my name is King
someone tells me they love me
and i don't need to unravel myself
to understand which me they love:

> *the black me*
> *the pink me*
> *the red me whose bleeding*
> *is not yet finished*

let it be known
there are no words lonely enough for
the estrangement of a body from its people
let it be known
we search for the words anyway
we find ways to reconcile our duplicity –
twice marked, twice erased,
conspicuous by our absence

crown me
King of a conquered people
King of a lonely people
King of a people so tired and holy
> from atop a hill somewhere the pink sun is rising
> and all the black children are ash by noon ↘

III. STORY TIME

at my first and last pride
a white man
told me and my black, queer, femme and trans friends
that we
(and our black- and trans-inclusive signs)
made him feel
excluded
...
...
...
how lucky
to have ever felt part of anything
how lucky
to come from somewhere
and feel like everywhere is a place
for you to belong
how lucky

IV.

dear god
forgive me my grief
that is a river
that runs into a sea of ancestral weeping
dear god
forgive me my bones and their unrest
i come from a people who have lain centuries long unburied
dear god
forgive me
i am trying my best

i was born into a pink sunset
under a rainbow sky
in a bleeding country
on a continent of bones
in the wake of a world drowning in birthwater

i was crowned:
King of the touch hungry city

———————

it's been so long

i want to love my body but
also   to disappear

          if queer dysmorphia were
folklore
          perhaps we would turn
into rainbows
          when we die:

                    a slash of impossible polyphony
                                        across the sky

          leading nowhere

the treasure was lost
long long ago

                              _____
                              (...) **it is a situation**

i tried to tell my lover all the ways
in which i am hurting
instead of each other's arms
we fell into silence

i tried to tell my mother about
the way my brain is eating itself
my hurt consumed all
the air around us

there is nothing this thing holds sacred
i touch the people i love and
they are heavier for it
a Midas touch for the internet age

i wish there was a way for me
to take back everything
i'd laid down at another's altar
take down the bodies from their crosses

and wash their feet in river water
tell stories that make even the dead laugh
i am not as good at this as i used to be
my sadness overcomes me slowly yet steadily

a remedy for crucifixion

there is a man
fearsome protector
let's call him the *Sword of God*
who lifted me from the floor when i was wracked
with a grief that unhinged my jaw
wide enough to swallow me whole
shielded me when i was
too young to know what
this life would mean for me
let's call him whatever name there is
for those who have given their arms
to the river

i dreamed about you last night, G_____
and even there i was still your damsel in distress
still leapt into your grasp given the chance
perseus to my andromeda
there is a fable to you inscribed
within the sepulchre of my skull
there will always be roses falling at your feet
i will forever be preparing a throne room for you
i will keep the fires lit for your return
i am glad to know that Love has many faces
in the sanctum of my adolescence one
of them is yours

archangel

more than to be memorable
i just want to remember

> the first baptism of drizzle
> the first smell of wet earth
> the first embrace and your skin
> like the rain-slickened road after
> the softest precipitous caress
> after so many days of drought

the way the hills would look in the morning
with the dew lying like a blanket of sighs

not because i have forgotten
never that
but i would like to remember as if
for the first time
to be humbled by the unspeakable joy
of knowing there is more
beauty yet for me in this world
if no other

i would very much like to hold you
as i did that night
where i couldn't fix any of it
but you let me hold you anyway
i would like to kneel at your feet again M_____
and take your calloused hands in mine
and listen to the meteors of silence
hurtling between us

at swim, two boys

ode to rupture
ode to beginnings
ode to the big bang within my ribcage
how much ruin you have endured

i heard on an australian comedy show
that the body doesn't recognise
the symptoms of
heartbreak,   or
grief,   or
loss
so it sends signals to the heart
to pump blood to survive
whatever trauma
has descended upon
its fleshen chamber
how wise, the body
to know that these things are deathly
to know that there must be an after
to know that these things can only last so long

ode to time
ode to survival
ode to the undeterred locomotion
of soft tissue and aortic breath
holy haemoglobin homunculus
hungry for nothing but life itself

heart, remembered

i go to lengths for forgiveness
reach a shoulder out of its socket
for penance
call me Atlas
call me witless
call me river with my
overflowing mouth

i've heard it said that god doesn't deal in guilt
i'm ready to get off of this cross now

give me time
give me the rest of our lives and
an open casket
nothing to run from but only into

praise the unceasing day
praise the weeping at midnight's hour
there is unnameable grief
and there is joy without measure

both are for the taking
or, rather, both will overtake you

give thanks
give in
give what you can and
give no quarter

jesus was once a boy

we must keep our eyes heavenward
for hell will always be there at our feet and
to name that which would set you alight
is to speak in smoke signals
sacrifice to the clouds

where there is fire there is glass
someone who lit a match
left a cigarette
in a forest now
aflame with neglect

betrayal is not always a decision
a kiss is sometimes a prelude to Calvary
just ask Jesus, or,
better yet, Judas
no one ever remembers to ask Judas

like a middle child or a pair of keys
he is always falling through the cracks
what became of him
wracked with a guilt that simmered
his body to ash

no ceremony
no weeping
a slow and silent dissolution
unholy penance for
a bag heavier than silver

whatever happened

I.
i am moving past / questions of
what living means / into questions of
how does living /work

heaven is not a place we can enter / without
the requisite labour / heaven is not a place
we can enter into / upright / but only

on our hands and knees /prayer
is divine labour
the meek shall inherit the earth / but

only after they are buried in it / christ carried
his cross / and now we must carry everything / he has
left in his wake

when the living gets too much / i bury
myself / in the work
labour is a way / not to think about

what death means / but to discover
how it works / mortality is the greatest gift
that eve could have ever bestowed / unto us

could you imagine
if the living
would not cease?

II.

in 2016 / when i was delirious
from insomnia / and ridden with a nameless
grief / a thought came to me in my deepest
suicidal ideations / the living will end soon
enough / until then / better to see how
it works /

my aunt passed away / i didn't attend her funeral
i didn't attend / to most things
i didn't attend to / the work
of living with grief / because
the living would end
soon enough

> i sometimes think / my depression / is a story
> i tell myself / to make the liv- / ing end sooner
> how to live in / a place where the / dead never die
> i want to go / home and tell my
> mother that i / don't know what / any of it means

> i want to go home / and tell my mother
> that the cross she gave / me is hurting my back / i
> want to go home / and tell my mo- / ther that she was right
> she was always right / and so we no longer
> need pretend that / we don't know each ot- /

> her anymore

i don't know what that means
i want to make this work

practice makes present

I.

tyrell alvin mccraney writes

    in moonlight black boys look blue

and yet,

some of us are rainbows

which means

    we are refractions of white light

which means

        we exist under rainfall

born under a half noose

in the ocean of the sky

    am i here?

    where have i been all this time?

is there a wor(l)d that exists

for me

that does not need me

to die

to become visible?

II.

i had a lover   once
they were beautiful
they told me i   was beautiful sometimes
i believed them   sometimes
i would make them gifts to leave
at the threshold
of their bedroom door
because i wasn't allowed in
because i hurt them
because i told the truth
because i know how to take instruction
because because because

i left gifts like a cat might leave dead birds
i had so much blood in my mouth and
i smiled
        because because because
maybe
they would see me
maybe
i would be able to carry on living
as though i had not become nameless   ⌐

III.
maybe i was never a person
but a rainbow
which would explain why
i was always disappearing

IV.
i can almost laugh about it now
or maybe i am crying upside down

(marco... ↘

v.
(i had a lover once
                sometimes
they wouldn't
let me
touch them   sometimes)

        i'm sorry!

i had a lover   once
they were beautiful
                once
i was there
i am no longer   anywhere

i am somewhere old becoming new
it rains here   often

VI.
i kissed a boy
                once
in the rain
in the new old place
with its old new things

he is so sad

we sat by the ocean
i read him a poem
i didn't finish it
we both got sick

this is not a fairytale

i buy him (sun)flowers
he makes me mixtapes
he makes art and in it
i am there
            a metaphor
but i don't mind
i hold his hand
we disappear   ↘

VII.

i don't think about rainbows
i don't think at all
sometimes i can feel him shaking
through the fabric of his shirt
i put my hand on his cheek

...polo)

we are both very sad

he tells me things
i tell him things too
he never asks for anything
which makes me want
to give him everything

i am not afraid of him

this is new for me
i kiss him like there is a sparrow
sleeping under his tongue
he's so beautiful with his eyes closed

VIII.
i missed the train
he waited at the station
he kisses me
and the sun comes out
we run out of words
and everything is tender

this is not a fairy tale

inside i am yellow
outside i am blue

the moon is shining

softly

_____

(just) enough moonlight

god
be a boy
be a bouy
be a bumblebee with soft feet
give me honey
make it sweet
make it true
make it last only as long as can be endured

god
let me be a window
let me be a sparrow
let me be a sparrow through that window
let me out into the free world where the light is soft
and there is a gentle breeze carrying me

homeward

———————

god as a boy

POETRY FOR THE PEOPLE

— RECENT RELEASES —

An Illuminated Darkness by Jacques Coetzee

Rumblin' by Sihle Ntuli

Malibongwe: Poems from the Struggle by ANC Women edited by Sono Molefe

— RECENTLY AWARDED TITLES —

Everything is a Deathly Flower by Maneo Mohale
FINALIST FOR THE 2020 INGRID JONKER PRIZE

All the Places by Musawenkosi Khanyile
FINALIST FOR THE 2020 SOUTH AFRICAN LITERARY AWARD FOR POETRY
FINALIST FOR THE 2020 INGRID JONKER PRIZE

Zikr by Saaleha Idrees Bamjee
WINNER OF THE 2020 INGRID JONKER PRIZE

AVAILABLE FROM GOOD BOOKSTORES IN SOUTH AFRICA & NAMIBIA
& FROM THE AFRICAN BOOKS COLLECTIVE ELSEWHERE

UHLANGAPRESS.CO.ZA